Uncommon Animals

WeddELL Seal
Fat and Happy

by Joyce L. Markovics

Consultant: Terrie M. Williams, Ph.D.

BEARPORT
PUBLISHING

New York, New York

Lost!

Dark clouds filled the Antarctic sky. A huge snowstorm, called a Herbie, was on its way. **Biologist** Terrie Williams plodded through the snow that already covered the ground. Her search for Seal 19 was going nowhere.

Had the Weddell seal slipped below the ice into the deep water? Soon, the Herbie would make it impossible to find out. Everything in sight would become a white blur.

Weddell seals are named after James Weddell. He was an explorer and seal hunter who traveled to Antarctica in the 1820s.

Terrie had been **tracking** Seal 19 for days. If she didn't find the seal, important **scientific** information would be lost forever. Terrie had no choice but to return to camp. If she stayed outside to look for the seal, she would never survive the extreme conditions of Antarctica.

Weddell seals are the only mammals, other than humans, that can spend the winter in Antarctica.

A Close Call

When the storm ended the next day, there was still no sign of Seal 19. Then, at midnight, Terrie heard a beeping sound. It was coming from the **radio transmitter** that Seal 19 was wearing. The seal was safe. She had survived the storm!

Terrie and her team shoveled snow around their camp after the big Herbie.

Seal 19, nicknamed Ally McSeal, was the first seal Terrie and her team of scientists **tagged** on their 2001 trip to Antarctica. Terrie had attached a tiny camera and computer to Ally's back. This equipment allowed Terrie to learn how Weddell seals live and hunt below the sea ice. It was a good thing that Ally came back after the storm. It meant that **data** from the camera and computer were saved.

Ally McSeal

Waterproof glue was used to stick the equipment onto Ally's back so that it wouldn't fall off in the water. When the seal returned, the equipment simply peeled off like a Band-Aid.

A tagged seal

Frozen Antarctica

Ally is one of many Weddell seals that Terrie Williams has studied in Antarctica. Terrie is from California and each September she travels to Antarctica to study these uncommon animals. She has been making trips there since 1983.

Antarctica is a **continent** that surrounds the South Pole. It's the coldest place in the world. The temperature there can drop to as low as −128°F (−89°C)!

Weddell Seals in Antarctica

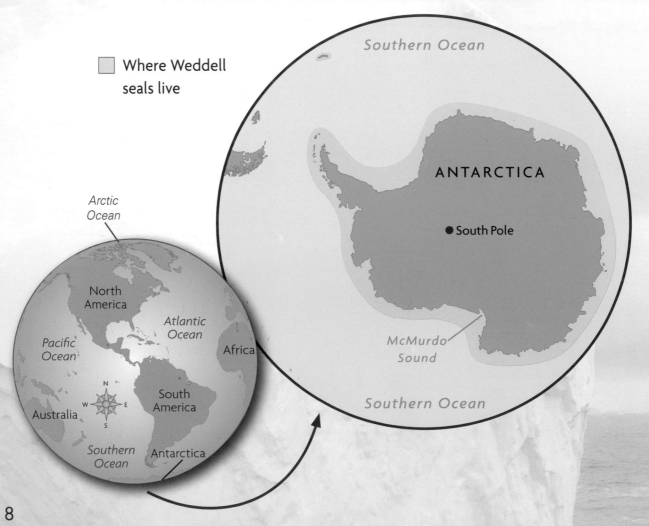

☐ Where Weddell seals live

Southern Ocean

ANTARCTICA

● South Pole

McMurdo Sound

Southern Ocean

Arctic Ocean

North America

Atlantic Ocean

Pacific Ocean

Africa

N
W E
S

South America

Australia

Southern Ocean

Antarctica

Terrie thinks it's amazing that Weddell seals "**thrive** year-round on and under the sea ice, without shivering and without long, thick fur." How do they do it? They have a thick layer of **blubber**, or fat, to keep them warm.

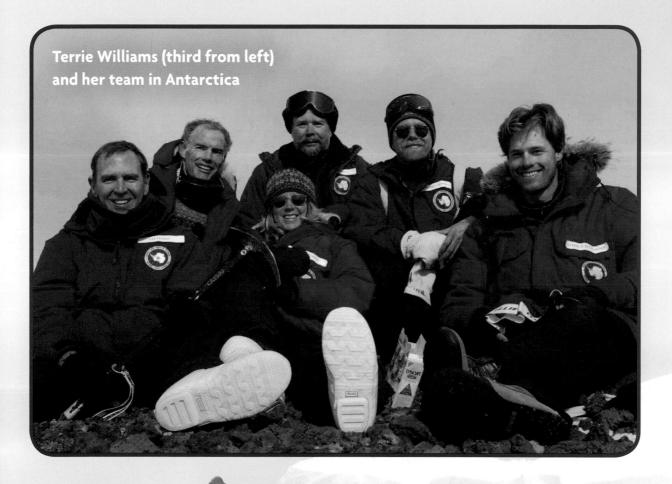

Terrie Williams (third from left) and her team in Antarctica

Terrie has found that a Weddell seal's blubber is between 1.6 to 2.4 inches (4 to 6 cm) thick. That's about as thick as a stick of butter.

Weddell World

The seals may have blubber to protect them from Antarctica's weather, but Terrie and her crew aren't as lucky. To stay warm, they have to wear many layers of heavy clothing and **insulated** boots.

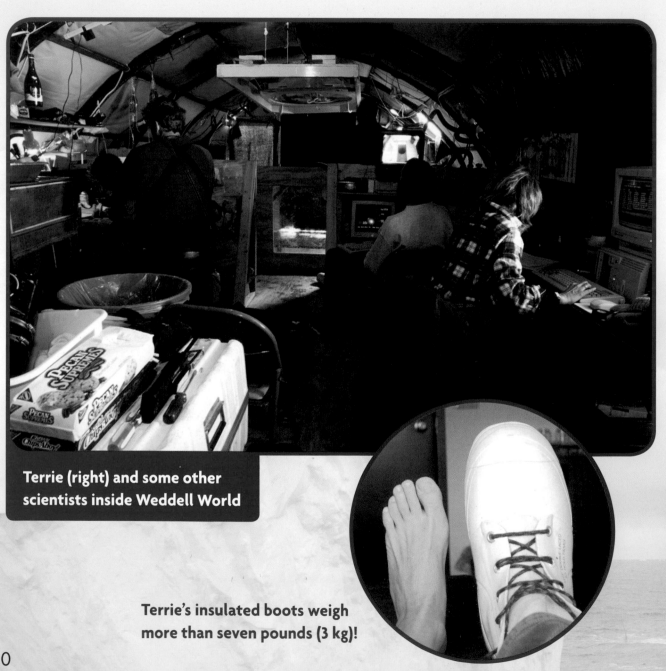

Terrie (right) and some other scientists inside Weddell World

Terrie's insulated boots weigh more than seven pounds (3 kg)!

The scientists also live and work in a special hut built to keep out the cold and the wind. They call their research camp Weddell World. It's located on top of thick ice that forms near the shore in McMurdo **Sound**. This is an area where the seals like to hang out and relax.

The seals are easy to find on the ice. They're huge and they move slowly. Terrie thinks they look like "giant sausages in the snow."

Adult Weddell seals can grow up to 10 feet (3 m) long and weigh up to 1,000 pounds (454 kg).

Master Divers

When the seals aren't resting on the ice, they're in the water diving for food. The tiny computers that Terrie attaches to the seals tell her how deep they dive and how many fish they eat. She can also learn how long they stay underwater.

The shape of a Weddell seal is perfect for swimming and diving.

Weddell seals can dive very deep—more than 2,000 feet (610 m) down. They do this by squeezing the air out of their lungs to help them sink to the ocean floor. For seals, diving "is like riding a roller coaster," Terrie says. "Going up takes a lot of work, while the trip down is much faster." Seals can stay underwater for more than an hour. This special skill gives them plenty of time to find food.

The Empire State Building

Weddell seals can dive 20 times deeper than a scuba diver. That's about two times the height of the Empire State Building in New York City!

Underwater Hunt

The cameras that the animals wear give Terrie a "seal's-eye view" of life as an underwater **predator**. She has discovered that seals are **specialized** hunters. To capture **prey**, Ally blows bubbles into cracks under the ice. The bubbles scare any hiding fish out into the open. Ally can then easily gobble up the fish.

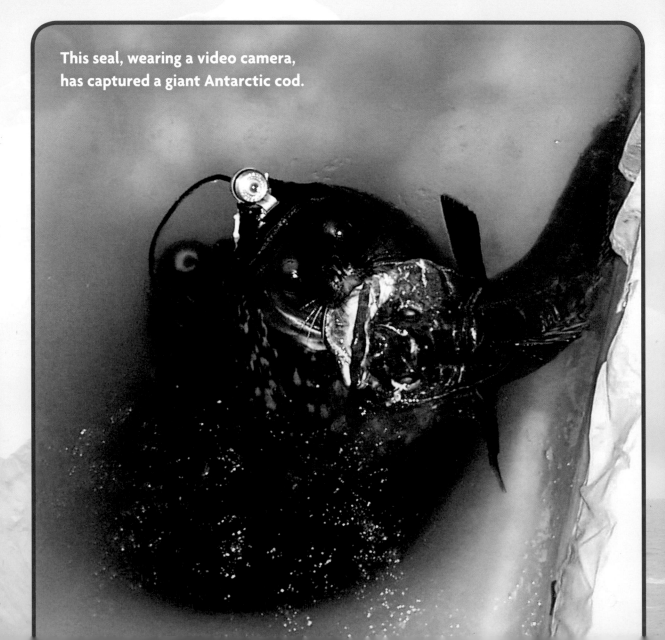

This seal, wearing a video camera, has captured a giant Antarctic cod.

Backlighting is another way Weddell seals catch prey. After taking a deep dive, the seals swim up toward the ice. The fish near the water's surface appear dark against the light-colored ice. They are now easy targets for the seals.

A Weddell seal swims up near the icy surface.

From the data she has collected, Terrie learned that Ally can eat up to 100 small fish in one dive!

Precious Air

Weddell seals are expert divers, but they can't stay underwater forever. Just like all other **mammals**, seals must breathe air to live. To do this, they have to find cracks in the ice or make breathing holes. Terrie learned that seals use their teeth to make the holes. Special forward-pointing front teeth help them scrape and cut the ice.

A mother and her baby near a breathing hole

After a long dive, seals swim to the surface to find a breathing hole. Sometimes they make a new one if there isn't one nearby. Then they take a deep breath and dive again.

Seals **compete** with one another for access to existing holes. When they really need air, seals will nip and bite each other to get to one.

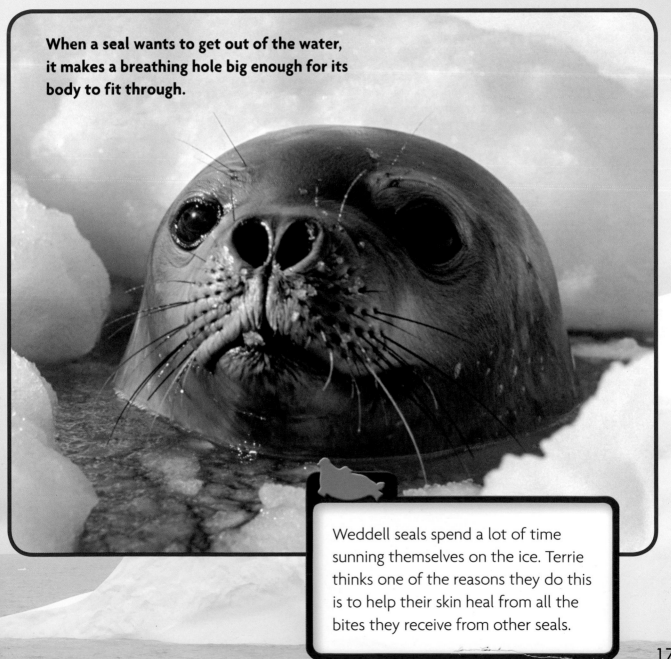

When a seal wants to get out of the water, it makes a breathing hole big enough for its body to fit through.

Weddell seals spend a lot of time sunning themselves on the ice. Terrie thinks one of the reasons they do this is to help their skin heal from all the bites they receive from other seals.

Music to a Seal's Ears

Seals make many sounds when they're competing with one another for space at breathing holes. They "chirp, click, **trill**, and create booming sounds," explains Terrie. She can hear them when she is standing on the ice and the seals are underwater. They're so loud that Terrie can even feel the **vibrations** from their calls through her thick boots!

Seals often "talk" to one another. They sometimes tell other seals to move out of the way if they need to use a breathing hole.

Seals can make up to 34 different calls.

Ally and other seals also use their voices to help them "see" in the dark ocean. How do they do this? They make sounds that bounce off the ice and ocean floor. This bounce is called an **echo**. Seals can tell how far away something is by how long it takes the echo to return to their ears.

Seals use their long whiskers to "feel" their way around in the dark ocean and to help find fish.

Raising Pups

Each October, most females give birth to one baby, called a pup, on the ice. It can weigh up to 60 pounds (27 kg).

Mother Weddells call to their young with special sounds. Seals know their mothers' voices soon after birth.

A Weddell seal "talks" to her pup.

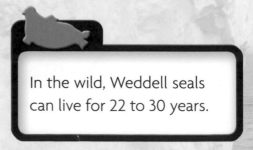

In the wild, Weddell seals can live for 22 to 30 years.

The pup's fur is long and either gold or silver. Terrie thinks a newborn looks like it's wearing furry pajamas. The special fur, called **lanugo**, keeps the baby warm. As the pup grows, it sheds its long fur for a short silver **coat**.

The pup slurps rich milk from its mother. The fat from the milk helps the pup gain the blubber it will need to survive and keep warm. After six weeks of feeding, and a few swimming lessons, the pup is ready to live on its own.

During the first six weeks of life, a pup can gain as much as 250 pounds (113 kg).

The Big Bad Weather

On the ice, pups and adults are safe from predators such as killer whales and leopard seals. However, there is one danger that can be hard to escape—the weather. The weather in Antarctica can change in an instant. "It can mean life or death," Terrie says.

A killer whale

A Herbie brings lots of snow and winds of up to 100 miles per hour (161 kph). These conditions are too harsh even for Weddell seals. Adult seals escape bad weather by diving into the calm ocean.

Pups aren't always so lucky. If a Herbie hits before a pup is old enough to swim, it can freeze to death on the ice. Often, mother seals stay on the ice to shelter their pups from a storm.

In the water, seals are safe from high winds, blowing snow, and the extreme cold.

The ocean around Antarctica is usually warmer than the air. The coldest seawater is only about 27°F (−3°C).

A Changing Climate

Weddell seals also have to deal with another danger—climate change. Earth has slowly been getting warmer over time. Higher temperatures mean that the Weddell seals' icy home is beginning to melt.

The landscape of Antarctica is changing as temperatures rise and the ice melts.

One possible reason for warmer temperatures is a large hole in the **atmosphere** over the South Pole. This hole makes the sun's rays very strong in Antarctica. Even in the freezing cold, Terrie sunburns easily. She has to wear sunscreen and sunglasses, or else risk **snow blindness**. Terrie worries that the strong sunlight might damage the seals' large eyes.

Terrie says that "a Weddell seal's sensitive eyes are about the size of Ping-Pong balls."

The ice that covers Antarctica contains more than 70 percent of the world's freshwater. If all that ice melted, the sea would rise 200 feet (61 m)!

The End of an Adventure

After ten exciting weeks, Terrie's 2001 trip came to an end. She removed the cameras and computers from the last of the tagged seals. Terrie was sad to leave the seals, especially Ally. However, there was a lot of data that needed to be **analyzed** back at home.

Today, scientists think there are around 800,000 Weddell seals living in the wild.

With their smiling, whiskered faces, it's easy to forget that Weddell seals live in the harshest climate on Earth. The extreme conditions make it hard for people to visit them in their natural **habitat**. However, Terrie hopes that through her team's work, many people will come to know the Weddell seal—a truly unforgettable animal.

Weddell Seal Facts

Weddell seals live in Antarctica—the coldest, driest place on Earth. They're the only mammals, besides humans, that can survive the winter in Antarctica. Mother seals give birth to one pup at a time on the ice. After it's born, the pup feeds on its mother's milk for about six weeks. After a few swimming lessons, the pup is ready to live on its own. Here are some other facts about this uncommon animal.

Weight	up to 1,000 pounds (454 kg)
Length	up to 10 feet (3 m) long
Fur Color	silver-gray with spots on its belly
Food	many different kinds of fish, including small ones that are only 3 inches (8 cm) long and large ones such as the Antarctic cod, which can be more than 5 feet (1.5 m) long
Life Span	22–30 years
Habitat	Antarctica
Population	about 800,000 in the wild

More Uncommon Animals

The Weddell seal is one kind of uncommon animal in Antarctica. Many other types of unusual animals also live there.

Emperor Penguin

- Emperor penguins are birds that can't fly. They can move faster in water than on land.
- The emperor penguin stands between 3 to 4 feet (1 m to 1.2 m) high.
- There are about one million emperor penguins in Antarctica.
- Both male and female emperor penguins care for their young.
- The female can walk up to 100 miles (161 km) from the nesting area to the ocean to get food.
- After the female lays an egg, the male protects it by balancing it on his feet. He does this until the egg hatches in about 64 days.

South Polar Skua

- The South Polar skua looks like a large seagull. It has a brownish body with white patches on its wings.

- A skua's wingspan is more than 4 feet (1.2 m) wide.
- Skuas eat eggs and dead animals, including Weddell seal pups and penguins.
- In midair, skuas will force other birds to drop their prey so they can steal it.
- The skua's nickname is "raptor of the South."
- Skuas like to bathe in freshwater pools.

Glossary

analyzed (AN-uh-lyezd) studied carefully

atmosphere (AT-muhss-fihr) the layers of gases, such as oxygen, around Earth

backlighting (BAK-lite-ing) lighting up something from behind

biologist (bye-OL-uh-jist) a scientist who studies plants or animals

blubber (BLUH-bur) the fat under the skin of a seal, dolphin, or whale

coat (KOHT) an animal's fur

compete (kuhm-PEET) to struggle to gain something

continent (KON-tuh-nuhnt) one of the world's seven large land masses

data (DAY-tuh) information, often in the form of numbers

echo (EK-oh) a sound that bounces back

habitat (HAB-uh-*tat*) the place in nature where a plant or animal normally lives

insulated (IN-suh-*lay*-tid) being covered in material that reduces heat loss

lanugo (lan-OO-goh) soft, dense hair that covers some baby animals

mammals (MAM-uhlz) warm-blooded animals that have a backbone, have hair or fur on their skin, and drink their mothers' milk as babies

predator (PRED-uh-tur) an animal that hunts other animals for food

prey (PRAY) an animal that is hunted and eaten by another animal

radio transmitter (RAY-dee-oh tranz-MIT-er) equipment attached to an animal that sends out radio signals so that the animal can be tracked or followed

scientific (*sye*-uhn-TIF-ik) having to do with science, which is the study of nature and the world

snow blindness (SNOH BLINDE-ness) damage to the eyes caused by the light that bounces off the snow or ice

sound (SOUND) a channel of water between two larger bodies of water or land

specialized (SPESH-uh-*lyezd*) very focused on one thing

tagged (TAGD) marked in some way to make identification easier.

thrive (THRIVE) to grow or to do well

tracking (TRAK-ing) following an animal

trill (TRIL) a repeating sound

vibrations (vye-BRAY-shunhz) gentle up-and-down or back-and-forth movements

Bibliography

Williams, Ph.D., Terrie M. *The Hunter's Breath: On Expedition with the Weddell Seals of Antarctica.* New York: M. Evans and Company (2004).

Williams, Ph.D., Terrie M. "Sunbathing Seals of Antarctica." *Natural History* (October 2003), pp. 50–55.

animaldiversity.ummz.umich.edu/site/accounts/information/
Leptonychotes_weddellii.html

animals.nationalgeographic.com/animals/mammals/weddell-seal.html

bio.research.ucsc.edu/people/williams/antarctic/Antweek1.html

www.afsc.noaa.gov/nmml/education/pinnipeds/weddell.php

Read More

Kalman, Bobbie. *Explore Antarctica.* New York: Crabtree Children's Books (2007).

Mastro, Jim, and Norbert Wu. *Antarctic Ice.* New York: Henry Holt (2003).

McKnight, Diane. *The Lost Seal.* Lafayette, CO: Moonlight Publishing (2006).

Sayre, April Pulley. *Hooray for Antarctica!* Brookfield, CT: Millbrook Press (2003).

Learn More Online

To learn more about Weddell seals, visit
www.bearportpublishing.com/UncommonAnimals

Index

About the Author

Joyce L. Markovics is an editor, writer, and orchid collector. She lives with her husband, Adam, and their pet aquatic frog. One day, she would like to snooze on the Antarctic ice with Ally McSeal.